DECORATING WITH

WALLPAPER

Victoria

DECORATING WITH
WALLPAPER

Text by Catherine Calvert

HEARST BOOKS

NEW YORK

Library of Congress Cataloging-in-Publication Data
Calvert, Catherine.
    Victoria decorating with wallpaper / the editors of Victoria
magazine : text by Catherine Calvert.
        p. cm.
    Includes bibliographical references.
    ISBN 0-688-14475-6
    1. Wallpaper. 2. Interior decoration. I. Victoria (New York, N.Y.)
II. Title.
NK3395.C35   1997
747' .8—dc20   96-33460
                                        CIP

Printed in Singapore

First Edition

1 2 3 4 5 6 7 8 9 10

For Victoria
Nancy Lindemeyer, Editor-in-Chief
Sue Maher, Art Director
John Mack Carter, President, Hearst Magazine Enterprises

EDITOR *Laurie Orseck*
ART DIRECTOR *Susi Oberhelman*
DESIGNER *Pat Tan*

PRODUCED BY SMALLWOOD & STEWART, INC., NEW YORK CITY

CONTENTS

FOREWORD

In the midst of winter a room can blossom with a field of lilacs; blue and white stripes can give the feeling of a summer cabana all year: There is probably no more dramatic way to decorate a room than with wallpaper. The possibilities are endless, as varied as your own imagination ~ perhaps a border, either to boundary a room's ceiling or mark your chair backs, or maybe a combination of patterns, with stripes to simulate wainscoting and a complementary floral above.

One of the most exciting things about wallpapers today is the renewed interest in document prints, making available to us the patterns that adorned the walls of the gracious homes in our past. These classics work as well now, lending the aura of comfort and timelessness we all want in our homes.

And many of us have very personal memories created and stirred by wallpaper. I still recall the little under-the-eaves room in my grandmother's house, with the sweet rose pattern on the walls. It suited me perfectly when I visited as a youngster and all through college, and resides vividly in my mind's eye to this day.

Victoria Decorating with Wallpaper offers all these different aspects, which we hope will inspire you to dress your own rooms with all the spirit and charm that wallpaper possesses.

NANCY LINDEMEYER
Editor-in-Chief, *Victoria* Magazine

INTRODUCTION

A room can be wrapped in color, bounded by roses, set in order with a smart collection of stripes ~ all determined after some delicious hours paging through wallpaper sample books. And never have the possibilities been so rich, as contemporary designers roam through the nearly three-century history of prints for papers to decorate a wall, choosing some to reproduce exactly, others as starting points for their own ideas.

Hundreds of years ago choices were limited, determined by what could be printed on a paper the size of a typing sheet and the designs the printer had at hand. Now we can pick from a lavish display of color, print, and texture ~ and often find the border and the fabric to go along with it as well. Where once a wallpaper was probably chosen for a lifetime, when a properly hung paper could last a hundred years or more, today we can afford our whimsies, our fancies, knowing that a change of mood, and paper, is no longer a big project. And because wallpaper appears throughout the house ~ snipped to decoupage a screen, wrapping boxes in a cupboard ~ it is a source of inspiration and a prompt to decorate the smallest corner and bring more pleasure to our lives.

Floral or formal, demure or dramatic, wallpaper's power to transform our homes has never been so exciting.

PART ONE

Walls wrap our world, and from the moment we began to build houses, we have decorated them. Though some of us live happily in a quiet white cube, content to paint and be done with it, for more than three hundred years wallpapers ~ whether grand and rich in detail or simply strewn with posies ~ have embellished the rooms that hold our lives.

Fashion may command a bold stripe one year, a pale and sandy textured wall the next. For those who like to pore over the great volumes of samples, roaming from era to era with the flip of a page, choices have never been richer. Take a wallpaper roll and a brush full of glue to a room and personality blooms, a personality beyond the power of paint. Clever use of wallpaper and borders can manipulate the space, as well as the mood, of the rooms in which we live. What was a box is transformed: Awkward corners disappear, ceilings lift, and furniture and curtains come into a

closer relationship than was possible when all sat marooned within white walls.

Once wallpapers were a rich man's whimsy ~ George Washington took it upon himself to order all the wall coverings for Mount Vernon, commanding neat papers in plain blue and green with embossed borders of gold papier-mâché. But when machines clattered into action during the Industrial Revolution, cheaper wallpapers by the mile covered workingmen's parlors as well as the grand salons of the wealthy. What had begun as fashion's plaything, a clever substitute for far more precious materials, by the end of the nineteenth century had become nearly universal, combining charm and utility in a pattern for living that set the pace for entire decorating schemes.

THIS PENCHANT FOR PATTERN

From earliest times, walls seemed to invite decoration: hand daubs in cave dwellings and the simple designs painted on or scratched in plaster walls. By the sixteenth century, nobleman and merchant alike realized that wall treatments ~ a swirl of tapestry, a carved wooden panel, a length of velvet or embossed leather along a wall ~ could provide insulation as well. In a matter of years, what had become a search for warmth turned into a quest for the fashionable as well, with design details reproduced on canvas or linen and hung on every wall. At the same time, printers were experimenting with pages of the black-

Wallpaper can be as dominant as the theme of a symphony, or as unassuming as background music. In designer Lynn Hollyn's house, the cream-colored curtains and sofa allow the wallpaper's bold blossoms full play.

21

In a parlor rich in English country
style, a fire warms a room full
of the artless charm that is created
when interesting objects of all
sorts ~ heirloom china, botanical
drawings that echo the garden ~
are brought into happy harmony.
The classic striped wallpaper, in
tones of butter and cream, unites
the assemblage.

23

and-white figures used to ornament book endpapers, which were easily transferred to lining a box or even a wall when the small sheets were glued end to end.

In England, the earliest piece of wallpaper known was found at Cambridge University on a ceiling beam, a simple series of pomegranates printed on a page of a book by a manufacturer active in 1509. Across the English Channel, several German castles were fitted with paper printed to resemble wood grain as part of their decorative schemes.

Only a few years into the eighteenth century, the English had disposed of their fusty swirling draperies and voluminous tapestries and were constructing handsome, simple, well-ordered rooms in which wallpaper played an important part. The Georgians had begun to paste the small sheets into longer rolls to make application easier, resulting in papers that, as a contemporary wrote, are "very pritty, clean, and will last with a tolerable Care a great while" [sic].

At first, customers ordered papers that imitated architectural details or materials like marble or stucco ~ expensive papers that were entirely hand-printed, for fashionables amused by the novelty. But eventually fine wallpapers, especially those manufactured in England, were firmly established in Europe and America on their own merits. Often a handsome border resembling a tasseled braid or a bit of egg-and-dart molding or even a simple swag of roses was added. Flock papers appeared when craftsmen discovered how to sift little pieces of chopped woolen

In 1857, when New Orleans architect James Gallier built his home, he might have chosen a boldly patterned paper like the one now found in one of the bedrooms, for Victorians loved the power of print.

A lighthearted room for a girl, below, is wrapped in a paper striped with a pink rickrack effect. Such a background lends a countrified simplicity to the sunny room, while the cheerful clutter of collections like those on the mantelpiece, opposite, seems important against the subtle stripes.

cloth onto a glue-covered portion of the paper, so the resemblance to cut velvet was improved. They were deemed good enough for the Queen's Drawing Room at Hampton Court in London (and they were so durable that some examples are still in place two hundred and fifty years later). These mock damasks commanded the attention of visitors to the best rooms; simpler designs found their way to the bedrooms, where the climbing vines and basic stripes that gained favor retain their appeal today.

MEANWHILE, ACROSS THE SEA

Americans ordered their papers from England and France, with agents commissioned to bustle back with samples and snippets and schemes to match the young nation's way of life. "Velvet paper I think looks too warm for this country," wrote Lady Jean Skipwith as she was building her house in deepest Virginia in 1795, and ordered a houseful of papers "of only one color, or two at most." The charming informal portraits of that century and the next often detail a family sitting in its best clothes on windsor chairs at the tea table, the walls carefully papered and floors laid with flowered carpets or woven rugs. The rich would order everything to match, from wallpapers to curtains to chair cushions. By the end of the Revolutionary War, demand was such that the American wallpaper makers, often recent immigrants themselves who had learned the secrets of flocking and stenciling and hand-coloring at home in England or France, were able to set up workshops and advertise in the local newspaper. Their carefully engraved advertisements featured tiny representations of favorite prints, and ladies of fashion poised as they contemplated their choices.

By the beginning of the nineteenth century, Britain, then France and America, had a bustling wallpaper industry. Paper was all the fashion, whether it was an English neoclassical print (which would lend a dining room all the glory that was Rome's), a French

Two wallpaper traditions meet: The print on the paper and curtain is an example of toiles de Jouy, documentary designs that began in eighteenth-century France and have been a favorite ever since. Below the chair rail, the fresh blue-and-white scheme is matched with a Lincrusta wallpaper from England, a textured paper prized for its sturdiness and subtle designs. It can be painted to match a fabric or print.

*Proud preservations: The couple
who restored this Missouri
house, a lavish home built for a
banker in the 1880s, knew
how to choose the sort of large-
scale papers that give a lofty
grandeur to a parlor, opposite.
The bedrooms, above and
below left, are covered in floral
stripes in the dark tones
that the Victorians favored.*

31

print brave with nosegays (for a boudoir), or an American design of flowers and trellises (the ones that decorated hundreds of simple bedrooms under farmhouse eaves). In the Victorian era, no surface was left uncovered, and walls in particular offered room to experiment. Up to three patterns combined to mark out a chair rail and a contrasting frieze above, with ample space for lively assortments of flowers and greenery to twine in between before the gilt framed pictures and draperies were added. In America, every wall in every house, large or small, paraded pattern on pattern. "What Shall We Do With Our Walls?" asked Clarence Cook, a nineteenth-century art critic, in an essay. His answer, not surprisingly, was to wallpaper them, wherever they were.

A TIMELESS BEAUTY

In a wonderful poster from the 1890s, itself the work of a wallpaper manufacturer, a woman in high Victorian style points an impeccably gloved finger at her choice of wallpaper, among cabbage roses and poppies, amid arabesques and scrollwork, all in mossy greens and vivid reds and oranges. Building a beautiful home had become woman's preoccupation, the choice of wallpaper setting the tone for a household that might be interpreting the newly popular designs imported from Japan or joining the revival of "Renaissance" tastes. By the end of the century, even fine artists and important designers were attracted to the medium.

Gilt medallions on a contemporary wallpaper echo the taste for special finishes that have so long been popular. Gilding brings formality to the paper; the rich green is a tone traditionally used in libraries, where warm colors set a mood for contemplation and for hours lost in a book.

The welter of machine-made wallpapers that called loudly to the popular taste affronted those of higher sensibilities, and artists and designers such as Walter Crane and Louis Comfort Tiffany, William Morris and Edward Burne-Jones made the treatment of walls the subject of their own talents.

It is not surprising, as the fashion pendulum swings, that the early part of the twentieth century saw a revival of interest in the plain wall, the white walls that in an 1885 essay were characterized as "relics of barbarism." To many, modernism meant minimalism: empty white walls, clean lines, one perfect piece of furniture adrift in an open space ~ and the technology was there, finally, to keep all pristine. There might be an interesting border, perhaps, at ceiling level, or a woman might give way to rosebuds in her bedroom, or choose a wallpaper for its interesting texture, like grass cloth or silk, but nothing more would have been fashionable.

As the twentieth century ebbs, wallpaper has been rediscovered. Plain walls have begun to seem underfurnished, and the potential of wallpaper in determining the structure and rhythms of a room is again worth exploring. We are lucky to have three centuries of wallpaper designs to choose from, with the freedom to adapt or adopt. We can be historically accurate, or borrow from the past in a less literal manner, influenced by the questions of scale and color and design that are all-important considerations when dressing a room with color and pattern. It doesn't stop

An early-twentieth-century house has been sensitively decorated to combine yesterday's sensibility with today's tastes. Our great-great-grandmothers would recognize the leaded windows, the iron tendrils of the furniture, and the flowered paper on the ceiling. The Victorians would have added two more patterns to the walls.

All lies in readiness for a new arrival: An heirloom crib is draped in white linens, and the walls of the hundred-year-old cottage are ribboned in pink rosebuds. Such a simple paper might have been used in this room decades ago; it brings a hush to the nursery and lets the rosy rug and chair cover stand out.

with walls: A clever wallpaperer knows, as did her eighteenth- and nineteenth-century predecessors, that just a few rolls can bring cheer to a storage box or a cupboard, a book jacket, even a mirror; wallpaper is useful as well as beautiful.

Surely part of this revival of interest relates to our feelings for what our ancestors loved, our curiosity about how they furnished the houses we still inhabit. Research has peeled back the years ~ and the layers of wallpaper in historic houses here and abroad.

Intrigued by the twine of a vine in a Regency print or a pattern the colonial Americans preferred, we feel connected again to all that has gone before us. "Why should the Old Time Wall-Papers . . . be left unchronicled and forgotten?" wrote Kate Sanborn in 1905, as she prepared the first study of the history of wallpaper in America. Now wallpaper companies plumb their own archives for designs to revive, and the borders, the grand damasks, the informal bouquets are again ours for the asking.

Though this old iron daybed and turned-leg stand are of the same period as the nursery, opposite, a change in the scale of the wallpaper design adds real panache ~ imagine the simple stripes here and the feeling is completely different. Papering just one wall in the room is an effective way to keep the pattern from overwhelming.

Scale in a paper's design contributes as
much to the mood of a room as
does color or pattern. A small bedroom,
opposite, is a patchwork of
posies and pictures backed by delicate
flower sprigs that echo the
scale in old needlework at the window.
Yellow stripes, above, are
scattered with a profusion of roses
that soften the geometrics
of the stripe and appear to widen the
narrow dimensions of the bath.

The restoration of Taggart House,
a Gilded Age mansion in
Massachusetts, included papers that
were historically correct as well
as warm and welcoming. In the bath,
opposite, a William Morris design
twines vines round walls and
draperies, then carries into the bedroom
next door, above. Morris took his
inspiration from careful observation
of nature, and matched it
with a reverence for fine craftsmanship.

Papers with energetic patterns
lend interest to an eighteenth-century
house, opposite, where large
bouquets warm the room. The purity
of the window frames and
wood furniture balances the boldness
of the pattern. The repetition
and moderate size of softer flowers,
above, set a more formal and
restrained mood.

CLEVER COVER-UPS

When, in the early part of the nineteenth century, a young lady set out on a journey, she was likely to bring into her carriage an assortment of bandboxes holding treasures great and small, from her sewing and embroidery to her best chemises. In America during the years from 1825 to 1845, bandboxes made of pasteboard and covered in wallpaper were the staple for storage, at home and when traveling. Some of the most handsome of these were produced by wallpaper manufacturers, emblazoned with their names (like contemporary shopping bags) and sold for a few cents. Still others were made by talented women at home, perhaps, using scraps from the wallpaper that had been installed in the parlor, along with newspaper or a contrasting pattern for the interior. Later, wallpaper manufacturers printed up special sheets in the shape of the oval or round boxes.

Today, designer Beth Ramsey works very much in that tradition. Always fond of vintage wallpapers, she had experimented by covering almost everything she could at home with paper, from the walls to the furniture; then she made a covered box for a friend. Soon she had set up her own business, Box Lore. Her little company covers boxes of various sizes with the old wallpapers she is always searching out at barn sales and antiques shops.

Some extra caution must be taken with these antique papers: As older printing inks may run, the papers should be cut

carefully; all the borders should be reserved for the edges of the box lids. When they are finished, boxes of variegated sizes and patterns can be stacked, giving not only extra storage space, but a handsome accent to the room.

Often a paper can be chosen to give a clue about the contents stored within: a pattern of buttons, for example, on the sewing box, one of dear old bunnies on the children's keepsake box, or dancing spoons on the picnic cutlery.

Beyond bandboxes, wallpaper offers lots of other ingenious ways to decorate and theme rooms. Imagine rosebuds on the picture mats that surround framed photographs. Black-and-white photography especially is warmed by the colors of a wallpaper pattern, which can act as a unifying element in a diverse collection of portraits and snapshots. A length of striped paper that coordinates with what is on the walls can be used to paper a standing screen. At one time wallpaper was specially produced in small rectangles that could decorate a fireboard or fit in the space over a door. Now it is the work of a moment to adapt a roll of paper to new uses. Even a sample book or two will yield pieces large enough for many applications. Wallpaper is sturdy, comes in handy widths and lengths, and is easily adaptable to cover a book or an album, to brighten a tray, or even to wrap a gift.

Any number of objects can be enhanced with patterns that are judiciously combined. Some rules of thumb will help: Look for a balance between geometric designs and prints, between the palettes of the papers, and between their scale.

PART TWO

hatever is of Art or Nature, may be introduced into this Design of fitting up and furnishing Rooms," wrote the eighteenth-century wallpaper designer John Baptist Jackson, "with all the Truth of Drawing, Light and Shadow and Great Perfection of Colouring." And, as the wallpapers of the past and present pass our vision, it seems that surely everything of art and nature has been pressed into service to decorate our walls, occasionally all at the same time.

Hyacinths will bloom in a bedroom, scenes of old China decorate a dining room, a plaid cheers the kitchen ~ pattern-on-pattern to suit a whim or a color scheme.

Originally, choice was limited. When papers were hand-printed, the print block maker sold his skills and threw in the design, crude or carefully drawn. Papers were, in the main, painted and printed to resemble what they weren't ~ that is, the colors and patterns of marble or flame-stitch or

stonework or even, in the nineteenth century, furled lengths of fabric and lace. More abstract patterns were drawn from the dictionaries of ornament that everyone, cabinetmaker and itinerant painter, needle-woman and merchant, depended on to set the shape of a flower, whether that flower was to be used in the splat of a chair or worked into a woolen pillow. The pomegranates and peacocks that appeared on beautiful Italian brocades were inspiration for walls as well, while smaller motifs were traced by a block cutter from a paisley shawl or a printed chintz or lace.

PERENNIALLY IN BLOOM

But as the taste for wallpaper spread and France, England, and America developed the trade, motifs were introduced that we still enjoy today. Perhaps the most universal is sprigged with small flowers, as full of artless charm as a schoolgirl's sketches. This sort of pattern was reserved for less formal chambers ~ the family bedrooms or inside a closet perhaps, where an inexpensive paper could be renewed easily. Delicately drawn, simply colored, and often contrasted with a background of small black dots, the papers are just the sort a Jane Austen heroine in her country manor would have known, as Jane surely did herself.

We never tire of the prints that are such amiable companions. Perhaps it isn't surprising that Laura Ashley's initial successes were based on reproducing these simple sprigs; with the Regency-era stripes that

A cottage deep in the English countryside is buried in blossoms, inside and out. When the owner wanted to build a bower of a bedroom, she found a rose-print fabric that matched happily with a subtle interwoven paper which acts almost like a trellis for the roses to climb. The room is small, but the careful interaction of paper and fabric maintains the peace.

53

often join them, they provide an adaptable background for modern living, too.

Flowers have their grander incarnations as well, whether they are flung across a Victorian paper in colors nature never knew or rendered with botanical precision by a Chinese painter or a French master craftsman. The urge to bring the garden inside was primarily a nineteenth-century impulse, when new inks and printing techniques allowed the paper designer to scatter flowers with a more liberal hand than the earlier small repeats. Though the very wealthy had often reserved a room for the hand-painted extravaganzas of the Chinese export papers that were so full of natural details, it was French wallpapers, the favorite of Americans after the Revolution, that set the fervor for the lavish flower displays that we still favor. Bowed with blue ribbon or poised in a vase, mixed with cool green ferns or backed with trellis work, flowers could fill a drawing room or a bedroom with visions of high summer all year round. Peonies and roses, larkspur and delphiniums, morning glories and buttercups ~ these are the staples of the English garden, and of the look we think of as English, though it all began in France. And during the high Victorian era, when so many were leaving the countryside for dark and crowded cities, the senses were refreshed by scattering rosebuds around the house, if only in paper and paint. Now a bouquet like this can be a choice for an informal room, be it old or new, in the city or the country.

Garlands of miniature roses in the palest pink complement the creamy white tiles in this bathroom, opposite. White accessories with tiny pink rosebuds confirm the delicacy of the wallpaper.

THE STORY OF HOME DESIGN

Page through books of prints from the past, and you'll find a catalogue of the enthusiasms of other eras, the pleasures of other times. What was in the news and in the shops ended up on the walls as well. During the neoclassical revivals at the end of the eighteenth century and during Napoleon's time, urn-bearing maidens and tumbling cupids with armloads of acanthus leaves were available for those who admired the Roman look. No sooner was Pompeii uncovered than the search began for "Pompeii Red," and classical ornament was clipped from the paper and applied to, say, the dining room. Toile de Jouy, the scenes of rural life that were printed on lengths of fabric, were equally appropriate to a wall. English wallpaper printers were not slow to recognize popular American figures like George Washington, who can be found, dressed in a toga, in similar up-to-the-minute papers. In fact, the French catered to the American market with a pretty paper on which simple lines alternated with ears of corn. In the eighteenth and nineteenth centuries, the taste turned to a rather Gothic style, and fanciful representations of castles and oriel windows were the choices of the moment.

Those who couldn't travel could cover their walls in one of the extraordinary French scenic papers like those still produced by Zuber. In these, a panorama of life along the Amazon or the famous port cities of

The charming paper in the Jane Austen house at Chawton, England, has been a favorite for two hundred years. This diamond intertwining is called a diaper pattern. Such simple papers were originally saved for less important spaces such as bedrooms and storage areas.

America was replicated in black and white or even in full color, in complex designs that required hundreds of blocks to print. Those who couldn't collect art could buy "print room" paper. Such paper came either in flat blocks of color printed with trompe l'oeil frames, with space to hold engravings bought from the bookseller, or motifs that included frames and pictures; both represented culture by the yard. Families whose houses lacked architectural interest could buy borders and larger samples that, with artful shading and coloring, could mock a marble balustrade or a plasterwork molding, or even simple limestone blocks, to give a weighty presence to a hall. Anyone unsure of his or her taste listened closely to the new tastemakers like William Morris. Morris brought a fresh hand to what he perceived as the overly dramatic papers of the Machine Age; he

In an old lakeside cottage atop a hillside, the rooms ramble in an assortment of shapes and sizes. Wallpaper envelopes each in comfort, with muted colors that do not distract from the views of the lake. This paper, with its bandbox stripes, is a close relative of the paper that would have been used when the cottage was built a hundred years ago.

produced a range of distinctive designs that combined careful observation of nature with a complicated interweaving of pattern. "Whatever you have in your rooms, think first of your walls, for they are that which makes your house a home," he advised.

Some colors of wallpaper were considered best for particular chambers ~ warm colors, for instance, in north-facing rooms. In the Victorian home, which was thought to be the repository of all that was good, choosing the proper wallpaper had moral overtones. As Catherine Lynn points out in *Wallpaper in America*,

If there is a favorite flower to scatter in our homes, it must be the rose, prized for the richness of its colors. Some wallpaper interpretations are as realistic as if freshly snipped in the garden, opposite; others are more abstract, dissolved in a mist of color, above.

"Manuals of domestic economy and decorating books argued that a woman's power through such influence over future civic leaders and prospective presidents was awesome, if not always obvious." With a noble representation of President Washington on the walls and some fresh ferns in the parlor, it was thought a child could be lastingly influenced towards goodness. It's comforting to remember that this era also gave rise to nursery papers of lasting charm; for more than a century, the frieze along which Peter Rabbit and his friends dance has never been out of production.

Nineteenth-century French paper makers created magical irisé, *or rainbow, papers with a high sheen. A reproduction design in the bedroom opposite and above was taken from an* irisé *paper that lined an 1820s trunk.*

Second only to rosebuds in
popularity, lilacs are as fresh as
an Audubon watercolor. In a
breezy bedroom, the paper pattern
provides the character; the
gauzy fabrics and traditional
furniture take secondary roles.
The simplicity of the color
scheme ~ white tempered with a
lilac that fades almost to
blue ~ keeps the botanical pattern
from being overpowering.

Harriet Beecher Stowe was as fond of pattern as anyone else in the Victorian era, but she believed in moderating the play of pattern-on-pattern. The sumptuous wallpaper in her dining room wonderfully illustrates the period's enthusiasm for Oriental designs.

AN ACCESSIBLE LEGACY

We are lucky that firms which span the centuries carry on, their sample books full of what was the rage in 1851 ~ and still in print. The Sanderson company has all the blocks for William Morris's designs and continues to produce them with care. The Zuber company in France and Cole's in Great Britain have vast archives.

Research over the last fifty years has literally uncovered the wallpapers of the past. Some sample books still exist, as do fragments on bandboxes or lining albums. More importantly, discoveries of scraps and whole wallpaper schemes still in place have given us a better idea of onetime choices in patterns and prints. Careful removal of wallpaper layers in old houses yields a vivid view of the passing parade of papers, moving backwards from vibrant abstracts in the 1960s and 1950s, through mock-Morris scraps at the turn of the century, to the rare hand prints of earlier times. These small scraps in turn give contemporary designers a starting point for papers that replicate the moods and manners of old wallpaper.

Firms like Schumacher, Brunschwig & Fils, and Colefax and Fowler now produce either exact translations, known as document designs, or replicas transformed by modern color for those who want to furnish a period home or simply summon up the English countryside of centuries past.

When Harriet Beecher Stowe
set up housekeeping in 1873, she
put into practice the precepts
she and her sister had proposed in
their 1869 book The American
Woman's Home *for making a
house "a bower of beauty." Today
the parlor preserves their tastes,
down to the simply patterned
wallpaper based on the originals
that graced the little house.*

69

The finely detailed patterns
of toile de Jouy are a favorite way
to wrap a room in charm.
In a Connecticut house where not
one window or door was
the same, the little rooms at the top
of the house were united
with the fabric and wallpaper of the
same soft, amusing pattern.

In many rooms, paper that takes a
more reticent role in the design
scheme is preferred. Broad swatches
of color on the walls of a sitting
room, opposite, are especially
effective by virtue of their individual
textures. The paper below the
chair rail is called Lincrusta, and
the one above is Anaglypta; both
were invented in England in 1877.
A bold texture, above left, is
appropriate for a room with architectural details such as a fireplace.
For softer furnishings, a more subtle
texture, below left, is better.

73

*Faux fabric finishes are
often modeled on moiré, above left
and right. These papers offer
more interesting backgrounds
than a simple paint treatment.Grand
trompe l'oeil swags of
roses and lace, opposite, echo the
curving frame of a Victorian
alcove. The iron bed was chosen for
its graceful curves, too.*

Documentary prints are at home
in a handsomely restored
Victorian mansion. The bedroom
walls are covered in a
print that brings to mind the fine
French trompe l'oeil
papers depicting gossamer draperies
adorned with blue blossoms.

DECOUPAGE

Scissors, glue, and some pretty wallpaper can be the starting point for the venerable decorative technique known as découpage. For this artform, motifs are precisely cut from paper, applied to another surface, and varnished to a glow. Dating from the 1700s, découpage was particularly popular in the Victorian era, when hours by the fire were spent cutting around paper prints and scraps which could be placed decoratively on plain surfaces. The application of many coats of varnish made the object look as if the decoration had been luxuriously lacquered.

Wallpaper offers endless motifs, simple or well-detailed, that lend themselves to careful cutting out with fine scissors ~ a most time-consuming part of the art. A fresh look at wallpapers may reveal the birds concealed in the greenery, the bouquet that can stand alone.

To begin, cut out the motif, using scissors delicate enough to follow each flourish and line. Experiment with the positioning of the pieces; build layers of design, overlapping and creating an over-all pattern. Using an adhesive spray, a removable adhesive such as rubber cement, or bits of removable cellophane tape, try various alternatives until you achieve a look with which you are satisfied.

When your design is ready, affix the cutouts with white craft glue or wallpaper paste. Smooth them with a barely damp sponge, and after allowing a day for them to dry, check for patches of glue or bits of paper that are not completely stuck down.

Mix the varnish with paint thinner. Apply eighteen to twenty coats of varnish to the object. When all is completely dry, you will need to sand gently with a fine grade of sandpaper between two additional coats of varnish. With a soft cloth, gently polish the surface to a sheen.

Frames, particularly those on mirrors and larger artworks where the design has room to tell a story, are good vehicles for découpage. Mark the center point of each side and lay out the patterns to meet at mitered corners. Look for a central element to establish symmetry.

A potpourri box strewn with violets in the bedroom, a canister with fruits and flowers that match the wallpaper border, even a chest of drawers covered in pheasants and reeds in the study ~ projects large and small can evolve from a good eye and a steady hand.

PART THREE

BORDERS AND BEYOND

We grow accustomed to thinking of our rooms as a harmonious whole, with fabrics, walls, paints, and pillows a thematic variation on our idea of beauty. Here, wallpaper becomes the leaping-off point, the prompt to follow a fancy to its conclusion. It offers a chance to dress the bed or cover a chair or thread a border round the room, to double and redouble the effects that we want to create until the room becomes a small, cloistered world of its own.

There can be little that seems as blank as untreated walls, those great expanses of space; even when it's bright with clutches of flowers or brave with color, a wall can feel as if it stretches forever. From the beginning, though, we have relied on wallpaper borders that match or contrast a main paper to carve out different dimensions in a room, and borders remain a valuable asset for fashioning a space. Running a border around a room at chair-rail level or lining the

point where the wall meets the ceiling can be like putting a frame around a picture, the finishing touch that brings a decorating scheme to life.

The choices are many. There are garlands of flowers that can grace the cornice; ribbons and bows, as if you were tying up a package; or a simple line of color that traces the room's architectural details. To top up a plainer print, there are mock festoons and swags, seemingly of gold-looped and tasseled fabric, reflections of some of the oldest designs. Those who live in low-ceilinged contemporary boxes, within rooms that seem all-too-simple rectangles, can add architectural interest, perhaps with a paper that mocks egg-and-dart molding, or with a deep frieze that carries the eye around the walls. A room that seems all angles and awkward corners, like a bedroom tucked under the eaves, can achieve harmony with borders that outline the pitch of the walls and the roof.

CREATIVE SOLUTIONS

Being confronted with rooms lacking interesting features is an old problem; unless you were wealthy in young America and could afford the fine cabinetry and woodworking that filled the very best houses, you faced plaster walls and beams overhead. Though for much of the eighteenth century the taste was for a wall of one color, provided by painted paper, the finishing touch was a border. Thomas Jefferson, who oversaw every detail of his beloved Monticello's

Traditional wallpaper and borders ~ framed to create a panel, ribboning the wall at ceiling or dado height ~ can still be fresh, opposite. Favorite pieces of pottery, blue and white cups, jugs and mugs, are amusing counterpoints in a china collector's house.

construction, sent to Paris for his sky-blue and pea-green papers, then asked for edging paper, festoons for the cornices, and corner papers stamped with trompe l'oeil curtains. Other papers of the time were made to resemble the architectural elements that may have been missing or, made of papier-mâché, added texture to fool the eye. Benjamin Franklin wrote his wife advising her to tack a gilt border round the cornice of the parlor. He must have shared his tastes with George Washington, who agreed that gilded borders give "a rich and handsome look." Though a chair seat might be chosen to match the walls ~ flame stitch next to flame print ~ when furniture was chosen to last a lifetime and papers for just a few years, the schemes were full of classical restraint.

By Victorian times, when pattern-on-pattern swirled about the room, a decorative scheme might have urged Japanese-style papers on the ceilings, a deep border of purple swags, and beneath that a field's

In a handsome parlor in Colonial Williamsburg, where many of early America's purveyors of wallpapers once lived, a new version recaptures the favorite colors and patterns of the eighteenth century. Neutral in color, formal in design, it is topped with a border that pictures stoneware teapots and cups from the restoration's collection.

A paper in a grand style
and scale might have been used
in one of the generously
proportioned rooms found in
a turn-of-the-century house.
Today, the small-patterned print
gives the setting a sense of
ease and intimacy.

91

worth of flowers; below the chair rail would be a mock-damask paper, and the room filled with curlicues of chair legs and rich red plush upholstery. Texture was as important as color and style: New printing and finishing techniques could bring velvet effects, iridescence, or even, by adding mica flakes, sparkle to a paper, and the border was perhaps the most restrained element in a room that danced with color. Borders might be naturalistic ∼ a band of ivy ∼ or gilded like the parlor chair beyond. Our modern eyes might find the frame under the full rooms more difficult to discover, for parlors existed to display the talents, the tastes and the wealth of the family who filled them each evening. They found nothing startling in a rug strewn with roses beneath a bamboo stand with leather panels that matched the mock-leather wall coverings in a style fondly thought to have been authentic Japanese.

ABOVE AND BEYOND

As this century began, tastes simplified when decorators like Elsie de Wolfe in New York, and designers like Englishman William Morris began to trim away the excesses in rooms and on walls. The love of wallpaper and borders remained, but it was expressed in more restrained treatments, with borders that lined panels of wallpaper, squares marked off in the center of the painted walls, and fabrics chosen carefully to coordinate with a general decorative

Borders can act as highlighters, underlining the interesting architectural elements of a house. A bold border marks the path the eye travels in a bay-windowed living room, bringing together the multiple patterns at work and emphasizing the sun-filled windows and their simple curtains.

93

In a little girl's bedroom, it's
all ribbons and lace, from the
walls to the dressing table,
wrapped up in a paper and border
that are a charming tangle
of green grosgrain. The borders
run not only at ceiling height,
but are doubled down each
corner in a subtle swag, like a
bow tied around a gift.

In this bedroom, above and opposite, a border of hatboxes marches around the ceiling and a scallop of lace makes its way around the chair rail. Careful attention to scale makes a comfortable pairing of small flowers and small stripes.

scheme. This was the first great era of the decorator, when a woman could consult with an expert on the rapidly changing styles, or keep abreast by reading one of the new decorating magazines. By 1906, a wise woman knew that an up-to-date room had plain walls, plain curtains, and the squared-off furniture of the Arts and Crafts school, but the room was finished with a deep wallpaper frieze at ceiling level, perhaps a forest of stylized trees.

This restrained simplicity seemed like severity to some, so it is not surprising that deep in the middle

of the twentieth century, eyes craved pattern once again. Fresh inspiration was found in the best of the past and through the ideas of contemporary designers. And never were there so many possibilities for artful coordinations, for creating rooms where all the elements related. When Laura Ashley topped her wallpaper of scattered rosebuds with a border of pink blossoms, her romance struck our hearts; it seemed as if suddenly walls found their rightful adornment once again ~ and the chair its pillow, the window its lace.

When Nancy Lancaster, the American who established herself as London's doyenne of decorating in the thirties and forties, moved to an old coach house in the country, she had to contend with a bedroom with low windows and a slanting wall under the gables. She covered every surface with a tiny printed paper, had the same print applied to linen for the bed hangings, then lined the room's cornice with a border that was a wavy line of buds, echoing the bounty of blossoms she had gathered in the gardens outside. What could have been hodgepodge became a bower.

Nancy Lancaster's print-saturated bedroom was hardly the first of its kind, though. Ignoring the natural tendency to visually enlarge a small space by keeping surfaces white can yield a more comfortable environment. Traditionally the French have treated very small rooms by covering them completely ~ every surface, from bed linen to headboard, from curtains to ceilings and walls ~ in the same print, often a floral, transforming any potential sense

A clever use of pattern and scale allows a rose lover to have her bouquets without being overpowered by them. Roses ribboning a side table are just the first gathering of blossoms; moldings frame panels of wallpaper like so many gardens, and the large-scale bouquets below the chair rail dwindle to tiny buds above.

99

Even a bandbox is covered in
minty stripes in a bedroom under
the eaves, where wallpaper
makes the most of odd angles
and lends the small room the
blue and white peace of a summer
sky. Matching fabric to paper
is a traditional way of making a
small room appear larger.

of confinement to a cozy contentment all its own. Furniture upholstered in a similar print is brought into a handsome union with a wallpaper that coordinates too. Even the hard wooden surfaces of dressers and tables, chairbacks and chests, can be painted with a motif borrowed from the wallpaper ~ a bit of plaid, a buttercup, a hummingbird. Paper and fabric may combine to mirror a texture, too, as lacy sheets find their echo in a border of printed lace, or velours, damasks, and moirés waltz from sofa to drape to wall. Thematically pure and simple, the reliance on a single pattern for every surface creates a harmony which yields grace to every room in the house.

The largesse of a room with high ceilings and wide windows is matched with a lavish use of pattern. The wallpaper blends almost imperceptively into draperies made elaborate with ruffled swags, and a cushiony boudoir chair. The simple two-color scheme ensures that the swirl of pattern will not overwhelm even such a generous space as this.

The power of pattern is
evident in a thoroughly modern
reworking of the traditional
cabbage rose. A chaise slipcovered
to match the wallpaper almost
disappears in the bunches of
flowers, while the punch of pattern-
on-pattern emphasizes the
decoration on the white-painted
Victorian bedstead.

ARTFUL PAIRINGS

Cultivate a taste for wallpaper and the only challenge in the end will be the enormous range of choice. Will you favor a paper that is an up-to-the-moment statement, or a document print that brings with it memories of nineteenth-century America? A bold stroke or a soft gesture? A practical background or a precious investment?

It is still possible to find original rolls that are fifty or sixty years old. Many of the new papers come with coordinating fabric and linens. Then, too, there are expensive papers made with hand blocks, as well as more common machine-printed papers. Sturdy papers are made to stand up to daily living, and embossed papers offer textures of their own. Papers printed with scenic murals envelop a room with sweeping vistas.

The first step is to contemplate the room before you. A few minutes' observation is the starting place, to survey the shape and size of the space and to gain a sense of how the room is to be used. "Proportion is the good breeding of architecture," wrote Edith Wharton when she was discussing the decoration of houses and came to the question of what to put on the walls. Proportions are still the first determination in finding the right match of paper and room, though the rules are less rigid than in Mrs. Wharton's day. By making the right choice, you will set the tone of the room, pull together a helter-skelter space with a small print or a stripe,

manipulate a large room's dimensions by filling the walls with a print in scale, lower the ceiling with a border, or raise it by installing the same print without a break.

Mood is the next modifier: Determine whether this is a room ~ and a family ~ made comfortable with an old-fashioned posey print in a bedroom, or a cheerful parade of animals in a child's hideaway. An important paper ~ with gilded details, perhaps, or flocking, or a large-scale design taken from an old brocade ~ will yield ceremony and formality for a room where guests gather, or a dining room where the table is set properly and the napkins are always damask. A historic paper will make antiques look important, a paper chosen for color or contemporary designs will make what is old new again.

For most of us, though, the decision is rarely simple, since wallpaper is considered such a grand gesture, and not one to be made lightly. We pore over sample books tugged onto our lap or, perched on a stool in a decorator's shop, we wade through a confounding assortment of papers, gently unfurling and sorting and rerolling them. Then suddenly, caught by a motif full of tendrils trailing sweet peas or snared by a regal parade of medallions on a background of the most sumptuous green, we triumphantly bear our swatches home to try. Plain white walls simply will not suffice any longer. We shall have wonderful wallpaper instead.

PHOTOGRAPHY CREDITS

1   Photograph by Steve Cohen

2   Photograph by Toshi Otsuki

4   Photograph by William P. Steele

6-7   Photograph by Steven Randazzo

8-9   Photograph by Toshi Otsuki

10   Photograph by Steven Randazzo

12   Dominique Vorillon

14   Photograph by Jeff McNamara

16-17   Wallpaper © Laura Ashley
Border © York Wallcoverings, Inc.

18   Photograph by Steven Randazzo

20   Photograph by Toshi Otsuki

22-23   Photograph by Toshi Otsuki

24   Photograph by Toshi Otsuki

26   Photograph by Tom Arma

27   Photograph by Tom Arma

28   Photograph by Steven Randazzo

30   Photograph by Steve Gross and Sue Daley

31   Photograph by Steve Gross and Sue Daley (top)

31   Photograph by Steve Gross and Sue Daley (bottom)

33   Photograph by Michael Luppino

34   Photograph by Toshi Otsuki

36   Photograph by William P. Steele

37   Photograph by Kari Haavisto

38   Photograph by Jim Hedrich

39   Photograph by Toshi Otsuki

40   Photograph by Steve Gross and Sue Daley

41   Photograph by Steve Gross and Sue Daley

42   Photograph by Robert Jacobs

43   Photograph by William P. Steele

44   Photograph by Tina Mucci (top left)

44   Photograph by William P. Steele (top right)

44   Photograph by Luciana Pampalone (bottom)

47   Photograph by Pierre Chanteau (top)

47   Photograph by Toshi Otsuki (bottom)

48-49   Wallpaper © Laura Ashley
Border © York Wallcoverings, Inc.

50   Photograph by William P. Steele

52   Photograph by William P. Steele

55   Photograph by Pierre Chanteau

56   Photograph by William P. Steele

58-59   Photograph by Jim Hedrich

60   Photograph by Steve Cohen

61   Photograph by Wendi Schneider

64   Photograph by Toshi Otsuki (left)

64   Photograph by Toshi Otsuki (right)

65   Photograph by Toshi Otsuki

67   Photograph by Steve Gross

68-69   Photograph by Steve Gross

69   Photograph by Steve Gross

70   Photograph by William P. Steele

71   Photograph by William P. Steele

72   Photograph by Michael Luppino

73   Photograph by Robert Jacobs (top)

73   Photograph by Tina Mucci (bottom)

74   Photograph by Pierre Chanteau (left)

74   Photograph by Lucianna Pampalone (right)

75   Photograph by Toshi Otsuki

76   Photograph by Pieter Estersohn

77   Photograph by Pieter Estersohn

78   Photograph by William P. Steele

80   Photograph by William P. Steele

82-83   Wallpaper and border © Osborne & Little

81   Photograph by William P. Steele

84   Photograph by Steven Randazzo

86   Photograph by Steven Randazzo

88-89   Photograph by Steve Gross and Sue Daley

90-91   Photograph by William P. Steele

91   Photograph by William P. Steele

92   Photograph by Tom Eckerle

94-95   Photograph by William P. Steele

96   Photograph by William P. Steele

97   Photograph by William P. Steele

98   Photograph by Steve Cohen

100   Photograph by William P. Steele

100-101   Photograph by William P. Steele

102-103   Photograph by William P. Steele

104   Photograph by William P. Steele

105   Photograph by William P. Steele

106   Photograph by William P. Steele

109   Photograph by Robert Jacobs (top left)

109   Photograph by Robert Jacobs (top right)

109   Photograph by Steven Randazzo (bottom)

110   Photograph by William P. Steele

A WALLPAPER
SAMPLER

*A portfolio of traditional and
contemporary designs*

FRUIT STAND

from
MANOR CLASSICS

A bright, bold
checkerboard

STORYBOOK CLOUD

from the
ZOFFANY COLLECTION

A simple design
shown in four colors

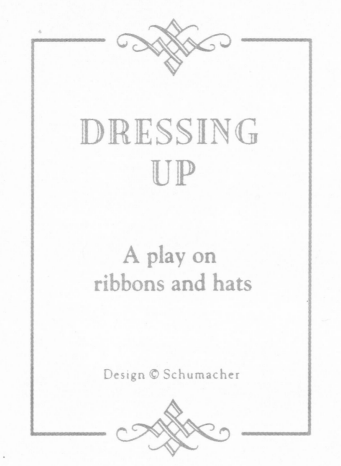

DRESSING UP

A play on
ribbons and hats

Design © Schumacher

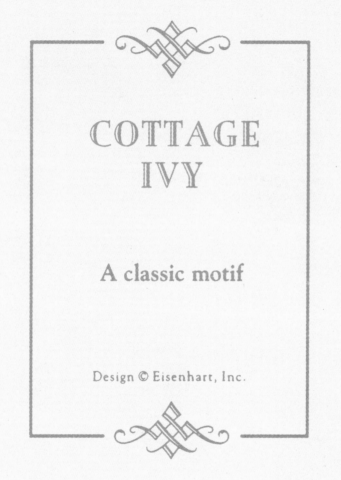

COTTAGE IVY

A classic motif

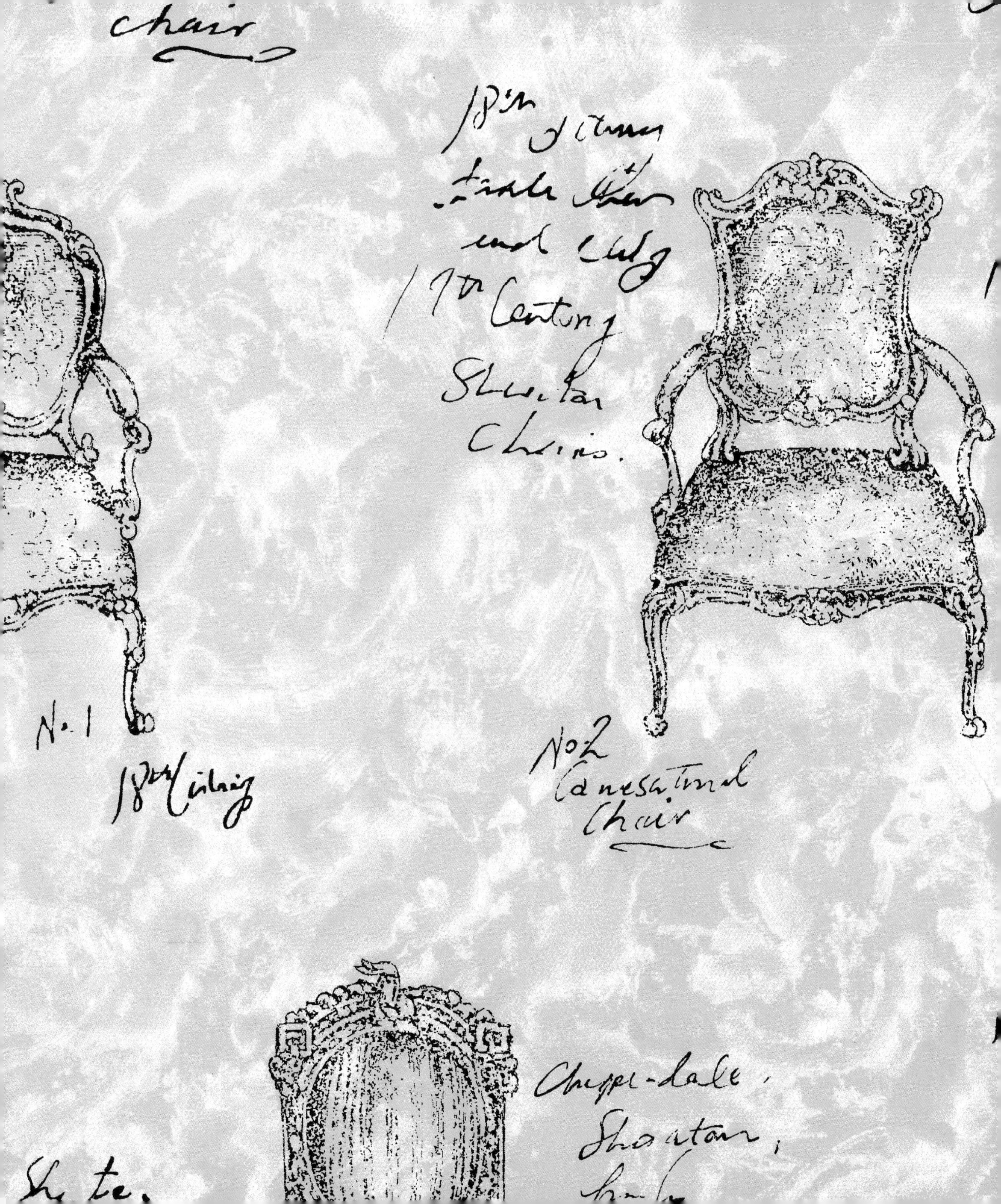

chair

18th Century
table chair
and chair
17th Century
Sheraton
Chairs.

No. 1

18th Century

No. 2
Canvestinal
Chair

Chippendale,
Sheraton,

Sh te.

MASTERS

Sketches on an
iridescent background

DAMASK BOKHARA

from the
ZOFFANY COLLECTION

A formal paper
patterned after damask

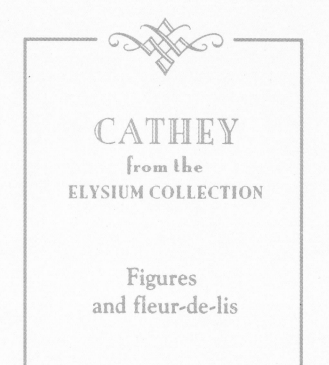

CATHEY
from the
ELYSIUM COLLECTION

Figures
and fleur-de-lis

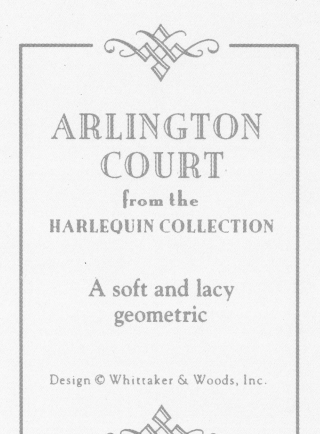

ARLINGTON COURT

from the
HARLEQUIN COLLECTION

A soft and lacy geometric

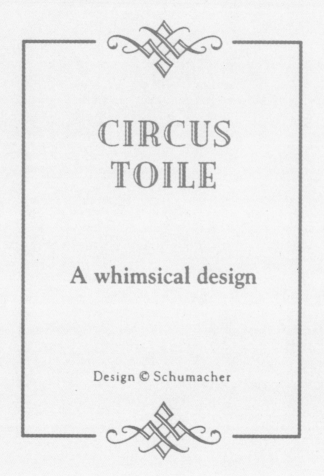

CIRCUS TOILE

A whimsical design

Design © Schumacher

GUESTHOUSE
PERSIMMON

Cottage floral

Design © Eisenhart, Inc.

SILHOUETTE DES FLEURS
ESPRIT DE PROVENCE

True French country

Design © Schumacher

ROSETTI'S GARDEN

CARNATION

A delicate,
traditional floral

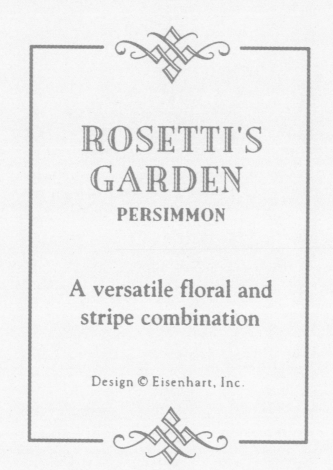

ROSETTI'S GARDEN

PERSIMMON

A versatile floral and
stripe combination

MOGHUL
STRIPE

Tailored elegance

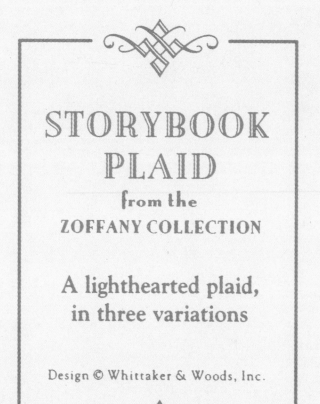

STORYBOOK PLAID

from the
ZOFFANY COLLECTION

**A lighthearted plaid,
in three variations**

Design © Whittaker & Woods, Inc.

TARTAN PLAID

An enduring classic